Pyjamas Don't Matter

(or: What Your Baby Really Needs)

by **Trish Gribben**

with **David Geddis**
and **Roy Muir**

designed and illustrated by
Dick Frizzell

JOHN MURRAY

Acknowledgements

Dr David C. Geddis MB BCh FRACP, Paediatrician, Director of Medical Services to the Plunket Society; Senior Lecturer, Department of Paediatrics and Child Health, University of Otago, Dunedin, New Zealand.

Associate Professor Roy C. Muir MB ChB FRANZCP LMCC CRCP, Child Psychiatrist; Director of Child and Family Section, Department of Psychological Medicine, Dunedin Hospital; Chairman, Professional Advisory Committee, Mental Health Foundation; Assoc. Prof. Department of Psychological Medicine, University of Otago, Dunedin, New Zealand.

The Mental Health Foundation of New Zealand.

A very special thanks to all those friends, mostly mothers, whose support and sharing has made this book possible.

0 7195 3710 X

© 1979. Trish Gribben
First published in Great Britain 1979

Published by John Murray (Publishers) Ltd,
50 Albemarle Street,
London W1X 4BD
Printed in Hong Kong

Dedication

Thanks to our spouses and all our children: Cathy (17), Rachael (16), Robert (16), Juliet (15), Robert (12), Joshua (12), Hugh (11), Matthew (11), Matthew (9), Christian (8), Andrew (7), Otis (7), Elana (5), Samuel (4), Kathryn (2) — the real experts!

Contents

It takes time to love your baby

There are lots of romantic ideas about mums and dads and babies that are simply not true.

One is that you'll love your baby from her first cry and she will love you; you'll all be wrapped up in a big rosy glow that somehow will keep you as a happy-ever-after family.

But it's not like that. It may take time to love your baby, especially your first when everything is so new and strange and sometimes quite frightening, when all those high hopes suddenly seemed churned into a mess of filthy nappies and sleepless nights and dreary days.

It won't be like the TV ads, with your baby all tucked up pink and peaceful in a clean and tidy house while you put your feet up or munch chocolates gazing fondly at each other.

It's not all lovely

There'll be times when your baby turns into a smelly yelling monster; times when you long to sit and not see the work pile up, when you wish you could walk out and be alone for an hour; times when the baby cries and cries and you feel frantic because you don't know what to do; times when you want to talk without grizzles interrupting, read and finish the chapter, knit without fighting for your wool.

It's not surprising that it's tough at the start. The wonder is that parents and babies survive at all!

You're not a machine

The trouble with being a parent is that you're a human being. You're not a machine you can switch to 'wise and loving', 'calm and understanding'. There's not another model like you. Certainly there is no way you are geared and timed to be a perfect mother or a perfect father — there's no such person, anyway.

And there's no way you can measure exactly what your baby needs to grow into someone you

You're not a machine

like. There's no set of switches you can press to bring out the best in both of you. There's not another baby in the world just like yours. You have to find out about each other as you stumble along.

For stumble you will, a lot of the time.

Feelings are catching

It takes only a speck of love to make a baby, maybe even no love at all. But it takes heaps and heaps of love and stamina to help that baby become someone you're happy to be with.

Feelings are very catching and the baby who soaks in love and good feelings in the early years is able to give them out later. If you can make the most of all the precious, close, happy times you do have with your baby, that's the best thing for her — as vital as food.

You can't spoil a baby

Loving your baby has nothing to do with 'spoiling'. She can't have too much loving, but often it's hard at the beginning for you to find enough to cope.

Think of it: becoming a parent happens so quickly. One minute you're on your own, then suddenly, there's a cry and wham! The whole world changes.

You're a mother, or a father! A new life depends on you, someone else you have to think of every day, for years and years. It's the biggest change in your life. How can you expect to adjust overnight? It's no wonder if you have lots of bad feelings with the good, lows with the highs.

Give yourselves time

Don't expect too much at the start. Give yourselves time to adapt to all the changes and don't blame yourself if you find it hard or depressing. The stumbles won't last forever.

There is no one way

We all get caught up in fashions, even in such basics as babies. Not long ago parents were scared to pick up a squalling baby before the official feed time; now you can feel guilty if you leave your baby to cry for a moment.

Mothers used to be unconscious for birth; now the thing is to find it a happy, natural experience and have the baby suckling before the cord is cut.

There is no one way . . .

If you listen to all the experts and neighbours and grandparents and talk-back callers, you'll be so confused you won't know which way to turn.

So why this book?

We hope to help you understand a little more about yourselves and your baby, mostly about your feelings, so you can relax and enjoy each other more. No-one else knows just how to handle your baby; you are the experts in deciding what to do.

But remember: Feelings are very catching. So if you know a little of what to expect and can have fun without too many fears and feel loving with your baby, chances are she'll be fun and loving back.

So much conflicting advice

What your baby really needs: Love

A hug means more than the exact amount of milk; cuddles mean more than a shiny new toy; being played with is better than being dressed up.

It's simple really. What your baby needs most is for you to be nice to him. When all the experts talk about love and security and praise and recognition and bonding and new experiences, that's what it all boils down to. Loving him.

Your baby isn't born loving you — why should he? He didn't ask to be thrust into the strange world. He has to learn to feel good about it, learn to feel love. You're the ones who show him how. It takes time.

And if you've had a rotten time at birth and hate the hospital, you may feel much more concerned about yourself than the baby. Or if Dad has job and money worries (or maybe Dad isn't around any more) the baby may be far from a blessing. It's no good pretending everything is always lovely.

Comfort and cuddles

But the closer you all are from birth, the sooner and stronger good feelings are likely to grow.

Everyone knows a new baby needs to be fed and kept warm. Comfort and cuddles are just as important; it's not surprising after nine months tucked up tight inside you.

Babies love to touch

Breast feeding has lots of advantages but one of the best things is the skin-to-skin touching. There's no reason why bottle-fed babies can't have just as much close nuzzling. In summer it's easy; if you have a winter baby don't always have layers of clothes between you.

Babies love to smell and feel and hear their parents — that's why so many stay happy being carried around in a sling.

It's your baby

Breast feeding and rooming-in, where you keep your baby close beside you (snuggled in bed with you if you like — it's your baby, not the hospital's, so you don't have to keep him in a cot) help you to get to know each other better before you leave to go it alone at home.

It may be harder to love a stiffly-wrapped white bundle that is brought in to your bedside when someone else decides it is time for a feed.

Money can't buy love

Whatever makes you feel happiest is the best course so if you decide to bottle feed, don't feel guilty because others choose a different way.

If you had a tough labour and feel exhausted and depressed (a very common feeling in the early weeks) and tearful or tense every time the baby cries, don't feel scared to ask if he can go to the nursery for a while. It might do you both good.

Remember, feelings are catching. Babies are upset when their mothers are miserable.

And when you nuzzle and croon and talk and stroke and have fun with your baby, whenever you feed or bath or change him, he'll start giving good feelings back — most of the time!

Terrible toddlers need love too

The tougher times for loving start when your snuggly baby turns into a demanding demon who seems to gobble up all your time and energy and caring — and still look for more.

When he's flat out all day making messes, spilling drinks, tearing into your treasures, under your feet in the kitchen, clinging if you try to escape, throwing tantrums, puddling on the floor, chucking his dinner away, grizzling when you talk to a friend . . . of course you don't feel great surges of 'love' every moment you see him.

But while you tear your hair and storm and shout, try to remember it's not him, but what he does, that makes you mad. Never tell him he's bad, that you don't love him, that you'll send him away.

Children need to know they are loved, even when they are least lovable.

Cuddles don't cost anything

Security

Security is a word in all the child care books. It really means making a child feel safe — not just from being hurt or burnt or run over, but safe from feeling lonely and unhappy and afraid. Of course it's tied in with love; that's the first essential for security. A child needs to know there's always someone who cares about her whatever she does, always a place she belongs.

Easy to begin with

It's easy at the start. All a baby needs to feel secure are lots of cuddles and loving care, food when she's hungry, warmth when she's cold.

It's best if the care comes from both parents. The more involved Dad is, the happier the whole scene is likely to be. Not just because a new mother needs lots of support — it's sad so many fathers miss out on being with their babies as they grow and strong relationships are made.

Babies and toddlers cannot cope with too many new people and places at once. They need a constant centre to their lives, care from one or two special people.

Cuddles, food and warmth in one package

Steady the wobbles

If they are given time to get to know people one by one, they'll be more likely to feel secure, to feel sure of themselves and able to be friendly and outgoing, happy to cope with more and more. You don't make children tougher by treating them toughly at this early age. They'll stand on their own feet later if they've had help to get over the wobbles at the start.

Danger! Toddler on the go!

It's when your child starts to get up and go into everything that the need for security — from dangers and bad feelings — makes things harder for you.

You must set the limits to what she can do.

Parents have to be like a guide-rail for their children. Not just to stop them from doing things, but to let them feel safe enough to set off, find out about everything, even make mistakes.

Try to make your house and garden 'child proof' so that your child is safe — and what is precious to you is safe from her. Then you won't have to box her in by saying, "No, don't touch, don't do that," all day long. That's exhausting for you, stifling for her.

No-one's afraid to be really firm if a baby crawls towards a heater. Try to decide what matters to you and keep "No" for when you really need it. A child will learn far more quickly that way.

Your child needs you to be firm some of the time — she'll be very confused and uncertain if nothing seems to matter, if 'anything goes', all the time.

Fussing doesn't pay

It can be just as bad for a child to be constantly watched and warned and fussed over, as to be ignored or neglected. You can see how feelings are catching — a parent who's always anxious

8

Security is a good trouser leg to cling to

teaches a child that there is a lot to be scared about, so she'll hang back and never try new things. Or a determined type will become extra defiant.

A fussy parent often ends up with exactly what they want to avoid: A child not allowed to climb in case she falls, is likely to have more accidents because she's never learnt to climb.

Off to hospital

Hospital can be a frightening place at any time. For a baby or toddler suddenly separated from parents and home, the shock can last a long time.

If your baby has to go to hospital because she's sick, ask to stay with her. More and more hospitals and doctors are aware of how it helps if a mum or dad stays close by.

If you strike a difficult nurse or doctor, don't give in. It's your baby and your public hospital.

If you know in advance that your child has to go to hospital, talk about it, take her there and show her where she'll be. Even if she's too young to understand fully, she'll catch your reassuring tone and feelings.

Let her take a favourite soft toy or 'cuddly' to be with her.

Of course, if you have other pre-schoolers at home you'll have to divide up your time. Try to get someone to help; maybe Dad can get time off work. Tell your health nurse of the emergency — she may know someone who can step in at home. It won't be easy, but do spend as much time as possible with the child in hospital.

9

Praise and attention

A baby who's beamed at for feeding herself learns far faster than one who's growled at for the mess. Praise for trying helps a child learn better than punishment for mistakes.

Babies and toddlers will do anything to be noticed. They need lots of attention and approval to help them over all the stumbling blocks of the first three years.

If you only notice them when they are 'naughty', only talk to them to growl, only react when they are grizzling, that's the kind of behaviour you'll get.

A child would rather be growled or shouted at, than never be talked to at all; even a smack may seem better than never being touched.

Babies want to learn

Even tiny babies respond to smiles and encouraging noises when they try something new — reach out to grasp a leaf, push a sheet away to play peek-a-boo.

From the start, babies want to try new skills. Remember, what may be maddening to you — hair being pulled, a rattle dropped 20 times from a high chair, a spoon shoved aside and fists in the porridge — is 'learning' to your baby.

Toddlers learn by trying

If a toddler gets a smile when he stacks blocks, pats the cat gently, washes hands, makes a road in the dirt, sits still to eat, he'll happily try more and more. He'll feel good about life and play away from under your feet.

If he can only get your attention by doing something dreadful like scribbling on the walls or bashing his baby sister, then he'll keep up the terrible tricks to be sure you notice him.

Toddlers need time to try things and make mistakes before they can get them right. If littlies aren't allowed to do things when they're ready

to try something new, they get discouraged, give up. Then later, when you think it's time they learnt something, they may have lost interest and refuse. That makes your job a lot harder.

Mum lands the job

The mother who always interferes because it's easier for her — less mess if she feeds him, quicker if she dresses him, cleaner if she wipes his bottom — ends up stuck with helping and thinking for her child long after he could take over.

If a child is praised when he attacks new skills, he learns amazingly quickly — though it may seem ages as you mop up the messes, correct the clumsy mistakes.

It's the trying that counts. Don't compare efforts with a brother, sister or playmate's. Don't ridicule or put down. If your child is good at one thing, don't wish it was something else.

If he's telling you something excitedly and tripping over the words, don't interrupt with, "Why didn't you wipe your feet?"

If he appears one morning in a back-to-front, inside-out T-shirt, forget what the neighbours think, and cheer because he's dressed himself.

Of course it takes oodles of patience, stacks of good humour — more than most of us have got. When you're tired or tense there'll be times when you brush his clumsy efforts aside, yell instead of listening, drag clothes on instead of letting him do it himself.

But remember, there are no perfect parents. As long as you notice more than neglect, praise more than punish, grin more than growl, the balance should work out fine.

It's trying that counts

Lots of play

What did you do that was fun with your baby today? Babies love to play. And they need to play and have new experiences to help them learn.

That doesn't mean they need posh toys and trips to town. It doesn't mean spending money and an hour for games together. It means giving your child lots of chances to explore all around him and to join you in the everyday things you do. It means having fun doing simple things together. For your baby, playing is touching and tasting and looking and listening.

So much to learn

Just think of the huge amount children have to learn in these first three years. Not only to walk and talk and feed themselves, but to know what is hard and soft, wet and dry, light and heavy, round and square, smooth and prickly, gooey and squeezy; what hurts, what feels nice, what moves, what stays still; how things go together, how they work.

That's just a beginning. They have to learn what they are allowed to do, how other people feel, how to handle things, how to concentrate, how to climb and jump, how to be pleased with themselves, how to have fun and share and think of others . . .

Obviously the list is endless. Luckily, children are born curious and wanting to learn. And it's great fun helping them — most of the time!

Bored so soon?

The good thing about helping your baby to play is that the sooner he starts, the happier he'll be. Even at a few weeks your baby may grizzle because he's bored — he'd much rather see moving toys or leaves on a tree than a plain, white wall. And the sooner a toddler enjoys digging in the sandpit, or dressing up, or pretending to hunt tigers in the garden, the more he'll be out from under your feet.

Here are some ideas to start you off — there are hundreds more in books, at libraries or play centres.

Babies love
- Feeling your face, grasping your hair, touching your breast, clutching a finger.
- Touching and gooing at a mirror.
- Watching moving clouds or leaves from a pram.
- Being carried in a sling while you put out washing, do the dishes, walk to a friend's.
- Looking at bright ribbons or toys tied round the cot or dangling from a coathanger.
- Reaching and grasping safe things tied tightly over a ribbon or string — plastic bangles, cotton reels, rattles. (Beware of bits than can be chewed off.)
- Sitting propped with cushions or in a bouncer chair to see what's going on, especially to watch older brothers or sisters.
- Lying on tummies on the floor with bright things (make sure they are safe!) to stretch for.
- Being pushed in a pram, propped up to see out.

Fun with Grandad

Crawlers love

- Mirrors at floor level.
- Paper or silver foil to crunch up. (Make sure a wad isn't stuffed in that greedy mouth!)
- Pots and pans.
- Plastic mugs, foil pie plates, cotton reels tied to a high chair to drop and pull up.
- Wooden spoons and tins to bang.
- Clothes pegs stuck round a tin to pull off and chew.
- Wastepaper baskets to empty.
- Daisies on the grass.
- Plastic bottles with rice for rattles in the bath.
- Strong supports to pull themselves up.
- Being shown how to crawl backwards down stairs.
- Balls to roll and push and catch.

Toddlers love

- Toilet rolls or cotton reels or toothpaste boxes tied together for pull-along snakes.
- Empty shoe boxes strung to make trains or cars or boats.
- Big boxes from the grocer or furniture shop to make huts or ships or to paint up for toy boxes.
- Blankets over tables and chairs for huts.
- Old clothes and hats and shoes and handbags for dressing up.
- Dolls and soft animals and old nappies for their bedclothes.
- Pretend games of hunting or shopping or going to hospital.
- Growing seeds or carrot tops in saucers.
- Mud and water for making mud pies and mountains and rivers.
- A kitchen sink with bubbles and unbreakable dishes to wash.
- Funnels and sieves and egg beaters and plastic containers in the bath or in a big bowl outside.
- Helping (!) with vacuuming or polishing or gardening.
- Hammers and big nails and offcuts of wood.
- Dough and rolling pins and biscuit cutters.
- Newspapers to 'draw' and scribble on.
- Bars or trees to swing on (with help close by!)
- Gates and fences to climb (watch out for roads and swimming pools on the other side!)
- Marching, jumping, hopping, skipping, kicking, throwing, catching, riding 'motorbikes' or bicycles.
- Walks in the rain.
- Soap bubbles and straws in the bath or in bowls outside.
- Scissors and scrapbooks and glue and old magazines to cut

13

Words, words, words

Even babies love words. And they need to hear words. Talking to your baby is one of the best things you can do for her.

Words are free, easy to use, always on hand, make no messes, use little energy — the ideal toy! Talk and sing to your baby as you feed and change and bathe her from the very first day. She is beginning to understand long before she makes the right noises back — and she learns to talk by listening to you.

Babies babble
Babies babble and goo early but words take much longer to come. Some say "bye bye" at nine months, others hardly say a word until they talk quite clearly when they're two. Don't worry if your child is slower to talk than the one down the road. Just keep talking to her about what you do, how you feel, what you're both looking at — her words will come.

If you have doubts about your child's hearing, check with your health nurse or doctor — the sooner the better!

The more children hear, the better. There's no need to change your words to baby talk.

Toddlers' tongue twisters
Don't avoid big tongue-twister words. Little ones love trying to roll out 'hippopotamus, haere-mai, wig-wam'. It's all good exercise for learning to talk. They love rhyming words too — hop, pop, mop, plop!

They know more than you think
Often the second baby arrives before the firstborn can talk. If the toddler is used to being talked to and given simple instructions it's an enormous help for this busy, busy time.

It's amazing how much even an 18-monther can understand — "Pass the pin, please . . . The baby has to be fed now, then I'll look at your blocks . . . Mummy fed you like this, now it's baby's turn . . . It hurts baby if you do that. You don't like being hurt, do you?"

Don't forget nursery rhymes
Nursery rhymes and finger games are fun to enjoy together and they are great for passing the time on bus trips, in doctor's waiting rooms, in shopping queues . . . The toddler who is giggling over, 'This little pig went to market', won't be grizzling because she's tired.

14

His master's voice

Books are fun

Do read to your baby — it's never too soon to start. At six months she'll probably grab the book and try to eat it. But she'll quickly learn to enjoy sitting on your knee, being hugged, looking at bright colours and listening to your voice.

A toddler used to books can amuse herself for quite a while, carefully turning pages as mummy does, pointing at the pictures. Great for early morning wakers! Of course there'll be some rips, so don't be too severe. Start with cardboard or cloth books and old magazines — your own example of careful handling is the best way to teach. And don't make your bookshelves out of bounds. Put precious books out of reach and keep the lower shelves for books to start looking and playing with.

Libraries have lots of lovely books for tiny tots. They are fun and free to visit. Drop in next time you are near your local library — your toddler will love it!

Make up stories too — you don't always need a book. Children love to hear about Mum and Dad or grandparents long ago, or myths and legends and fairy tales told in your words.

Knowing (roughly) a little of what to expect

Hardly anyone would smack a baby who bumps a drink or can't hold a spoon properly (sadly, some parents do). It's just as silly to expect a toddler to sit still and quiet while you chat on the phone. Or to growl at an 18-monther for wet pants. Or to despair if your toddler insists on doing something his way. All children go through stages as they grow; not only the sitting, crawling, walking stages but behaviour changes that are just as important. Often these swing between the 'good' and the 'bad', between smiley, sunny, wanting-to-please stages and grizzley, stormy, stubborn, 'no-I-won't' stages.

Knowing a little of what to expect doesn't mean you do nothing about the 'nasty' bits. But, hopefully, knowing they are normal helps you to handle them in an understanding, relaxed way, without blaming yourself for being a 'bad' parent or your child for being 'naughty' long before he is capable of deliberate naughtiness.

No-one can tell you exactly when your baby will go through certain phases — they differ with every child. The timing isn't so important. But at every stage your child is finding out or feeling something new about himself and the world around him. Each discovery is important — even the difficult 'no-I-won't' times when a toddler learns he is a person who can do things for himself and starts learning the limits, that there are some things he is not allowed to do.

Don't be scared you'll be stuck with a monster for life when things are rough with a 1½ or 2½-year-old. There are times when littlies can be

hell to live with. Whatever he's doing, if you can help, then steer him round the thorny patches, it won't last! Don't expect too much too soon.

Here's a guide to some of those stages:

Baby (up to 9 months)

- Helpless and completely dependent on you. Cries, sucks and sleeps. Doesn't know night from day. Needs constant loving care; can't be 'spoilt' or 'trained' or learn to wait at this early stage.
- May cry a lot at a particular time, usually at the end of day (P 20). Starts to smile, coo, chuckle. Discovers thumb and fingers to suck or play with.
- May get bored or lonely. Likes being propped up with cushions or bouncer chair to watch family happenings. Likes bright moving things to watch (P 12).
- Settles into a routine, starts sleeping through the night (P 22).
- Starts grasping things, sitting up, eating with fingers, droppingthings from cot or high chair.
- Likes to kick with no nappies on, to 'swim' on tummy on the floor, to reach for playthings, play peek-a-boo (P 12).
- Babbles and goos and loves being talked to (P 14).
- Puts everything in mouth — beware of tiny objects or toys that can be chewed or come to pieces.
- May by shy of strangers, cry when Mum or Dad leaves.

Crawler (up to 18 months)

- Into everything. Wants (and needs) to explore, so lock up toilet cleaner, detergent and kitchen cleaners, poisons, medicine and beware of pills in visitors' handbags. Put precious breakables up high or put catches on some cupboards. But leave the saucepan cupboard open — a favourite place.
- Gets restless in a play pen, needs plenty to play with and loves throwing things for you to return (P13).
- Enjoys picture books and simple stories (P15).
- Learns to wave "bye bye" and smile when you leave — or may still cling and be shy.
- Starts to fuss, dawdle and refuse food (P28).
- Starts wanting to do things his way or by himself. Resists being washed, dressed, helped to eat. May yell violently if he can't have his way or when he can't tell you what he wants, but is easily diverted with a game or toy or something to look at.
- May sit on potty but generally is too young to be trained, especially boys (P30).
- Starts to understand a firm "No" but will keep on with touching or annoying tricks. Needs firm "No" and physical removal from heaters, TV knobs, etc. — offer something else to distract. Try to keep "No" for essentials (P32).
- Disturbed sleeping, wakes very early (P22).
- Loves to play in sand, mud, water — a very messy, very important stage (P13).
- Understands far more words than he can say. At times will follow simple requests like, "Pass the pin please", "Get your coat", but will often do the opposite of what you want. Has learnt to wait a little but has no idea of "hurry", "soon", "later", "her turn" (P14).

Toddler (up to 3 years)

- See-saws between willing-to-please, affectionate moods or stages and stubborn, do-it-my-way, rejecting stages. Goes through calm then stormy patches. Flat out, exploring, learning, playing. Needs constant watching, especially from roads, rivers, pools, deep drains or puddles, at the sea, near heaters, fires, cooking. Parents need all the patience and good nature they can find to try to forestall trouble — you can't force a toddler to be "good". An exhausting age, but lots of fun!
- May have tantrums, even over minor things (P34).
- Likes to "help" at the sink, vacuuming, gardening. Breaks and spills through clumsiness, not naughtiness.
- Moves stools or boxes to climb up, wants to reach for himself, pour own drinks, etc. — very messy! Check that poisons and precious bits are high enough.
- Starts (around two) telling you if pants are wet or dirty. Learns to use a pot though accidents happen at any time (P30).
- Often seems to live on fresh air, eats very little. Feeds himself, can't cope with table manners (P26).
- Seems to delight in doing the opposite of what you want: Runs away when called, shrieks or grizzles when you want quiet, especially while you telephone, wants a pink mug when you give the red.
- May want to choose clothes or change them all through a day.
- Can't sit still for long. Likes to jump, run, swing on arms, learn to skip, hop, throw and catch balls (P13).

- At times (around 2½) very persistent, hard to budge. Likes things done a certain way, especially bedtime rituals (P24), unhappy about even little changes.
- May be very attached to a cuddly or favourite toy.
- May seem to go backwards, especially if there have been upsets or changes (parents moving house, separating, new baby arriving, etc.). May cling and cry when left, wet pants again, wake at nights (P38).
- Learns to talk and keeps up non-stop chatter. Favourite word is often "No". Understands far more than he can say and needs lots of talking and listening to (P14).
- Likes books being read or looking at pictures by himself.
- Asks endless questions that shouldn't be brushed aside.
- May happily go off to play at friend's, or be left with minder, then grizzle and cling when Mum returns (P44).
- Enjoys playing with friends, needs time to learn to share (P37).
- Loves make-believe play, dressing up, inventing people or animals in the garden (P13).

Chatter, chatter, chatter

19

Why does he cry?

All babies cry. And all mothers at times feel frantic about it.

Some babies cry very little; others seem to cry endlessly. It varies enormously from baby to baby.

A way of talking
Crying is a baby's way of talking. Learning to read the signals he sends with his cries is what the early weeks with a new baby are all about.

Often it's hard, especially for a new mother listening to the fierce wails of her first baby. You cannot hope to interpret them all.

Is he hungry? Or has he got wind? Is he too hot, too cold? Tucked in too tight? Too loose? Dirty nappies? Pricked by a pin? The list seems endless and when you've checked everything it seems time to start again!

A baby's cry has a very marked effect on his own mother. Often a mother can pick her baby's cry from a noisy nursery. One whimper in the night and a mum who sleeps through TV gun battles will be wide awake. A breast-feeding mother sometimes spurts milk when her baby cries. Hot prickly feelings of anger or panic can be triggered when your own baby cries — while any other infant's squalling leaves you cool and calm.

Switched on
It's natural that you react strongly. It's one of the ways you learn to switch on to what your baby needs. And it's no wonder when he cries and you don't know the reason that you get upset.

There's a lot of nonsense talked about crying: That it 'exercises' the baby's lungs, that a 'good' baby never cries (how can a baby be 'bad'?), that you'll create a bad habit if you pick up your baby when he cries, or the opposite — that you must never let him cry.

Babies can't be 'spoiled'
Neglect, or trying far too soon to 'train' a baby into a pattern that suits you and not him may 'spoil' an infant. Certainly you won't spoil him by picking him up when he cries.

The less a baby is left to cry, the less he's likely to cry. If he's quickly comforted with holding and feeding when he's distressed by loneliness or hunger, he learns that he doesn't need to shout and yell for attention. He's likely to be less (not more) demanding once he settles into a routine.

Hunger is the commonest cause of crying in the early weeks. But loneliness may be just as big a reason. To be suddenly alone and apart in a cot must seem frightening at times. Comfort for a baby is being held close to the skin he knows — that's better than the poshest cot in the land!

The more Dad can be the comforter from the beginning the more it will start good feelings between him and his baby — and lighten the load on Mum.

Bored already?
Boredom can be a reason for crying sooner than you expect. Even from a few weeks old babies like to have bright moving things to look at, or to be near the family action. That's why carrying a baby in a sling while you do ordinary things keeps him content and amused.

Don't blame yourself
Prolonged crying bouts are especially upsetting for new mothers because they often blame themselves: "What's wrong with me that the baby cries?" instead of, "What's wrong with the baby?" Lots of babies have crying times when nothing seems to comfort them. Usually it's at the end of the day, just when you're busiest and tired, and least able to stay calm about the

You can't hope to understand every cry

crying. A yowling baby then can be ghastly, absolute hell.

You matter

If your baby goes on crying after you've checked everything you can think of, it's normal that you feel desperate about the noise. Remember, *you* matter. If you let yourself get frantic and worn to a frazzle, it doesn't help anyone, least of all the baby who will pick up your tense feelings.

There are times when the best thing to do is simply walk away. Leave the baby. Shut the door. Get out of earshot. Have a drink, turn some music up to drown out the sound. Best of all, turn the baby over to Dad or a friend and let them cope — they won't be feeling all on edge like you. Go for a walk to calm down.

Upset mother: upset baby

If your baby seems to cry an awful lot, do tell your nurse or doctor about it. Maybe you are more tense or depressed than you let on and the baby is catching those feelings. Or maybe your baby is one who just cries a lot, and of course this makes you upset. Let yourself be helped if you have family or friends who offer to give you a break. Babies who cry a lot usually stop after the first three months. It's really not long but it seems ages while it lasts. This may be a most important time to get a baby-sitter to take the pressure off.

Dummy

Thumbs and fingers are the natural comforter for baby (X-rays show babies thumb-sucking in the womb!) and have the advantage of being able to feel and help a baby explore his mouth, finding pleasure in his own body. Never dip a dummy in honey or sweetener. Sugar ruins new teeth while they are forming. If an older baby wants his dummy all the time maybe he isn't getting enough of your attention or other good things to do.

Wind

Wind is blamed for baby's crying when no-one really knows what the matter is. As long as he's had time to sit on your lap or been held over your shoulder after a feed you needn't keep trying to bring up a burp — it's often greatly overdone.

Teething

After three or four months, it's common to stop blaming wind for crying and start on teething, but again it is often just a handy label when no-one knows why baby is grizzley. Some babies are irritable before a tooth comes through and like safe, cold things to chew on. Teething doesn't make a baby sick so if you are worried ask your nurse or doctor.

Why doesn't she sleep?

There's no way you can force a wide-awake baby to sleep — but it's very common for parents to try!

It's normal for a baby who has been sleeping through the night to suddenly start yelling at odd hours. *It's normal* for a toddler to wake at midnight and want to talk and play. *It's normal* for junior to be ready to start the day at 5 am . . . And it's perfectly natural that parents don't like these things!

Most children, in their first three years, go through stages of disturbed sleep. It's tough for parents — one of the hardest things you have to cope with.

There's no magic answer to sleep problems. No-one really knows why children wake in the night after the first settling-in weeks. Often there's nothing much you can do except grin and bear it and remind yourself your baby didn't ask to be born; you can't expect her not to interfere with your life.

It's you who needs the sleep
Problems start because most children need less sleep than parents want them to have. People used to think that babies grew only while they slept. Sleep was measured rigidly — so many hours were considered vital for every age. This is not true. Every child varies in his sleep needs, right from the start.

Let's be honest: We want children to sleep all night for our sake, not just for theirs. We need the rest from them. It's impossible to keep going 24 hours a day.

Trying to force a child to sleep starts battles which you are bound to lose.

You can't control the amount your child sleeps. But you can influence her attitude towards bed:

What you can do
• with babies
A new baby takes time to settle into a sleeping pattern but be assured she'll sleep when tired and there's no need to add up her sleeping hours.

Tiny babies don't know night from day and need to be fed when they wake in the night. Some take much longer than others to drop the night feeds — there's no way you can 'train' your baby into staying asleep and not calling for food when she's hungry.

Rocking and singing or carrying a baby in a sling often helps to soothe her off to sleep and you need have no fears of starting bad patterns in these early weeks.

Start giving the message that nights are for sleeping by being quieter and quicker with the night feeds. As soon as you've fed and changed and soothed the baby, tuck her back in her cot. She'll begin to learn there are no prizes for waking sleepy parents.

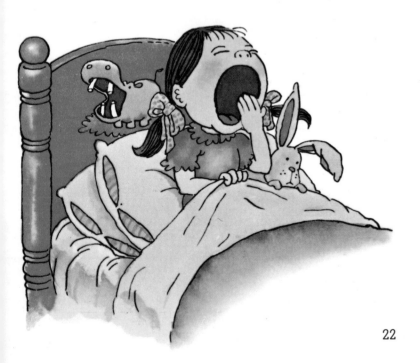

She may start crying the minute you put her down — of course, she'd rather be in your arms! But remember, you're not a machine. You need that sleep. The testing cry probably won't last long if you give her a chance to settle.

Snuggling the new baby in bed beside you can be a good way of coping with the early up-and-down nights and you needn't be scared of squashing her — babies can wriggle when they want to.

While night feeds are on, it's easier to have baby in your room. But if there's another bedroom it's a good idea to move her there after the early settling-in weeks. An alert three or four-monther who hears parents in the night will naturally want to be with them. And if you hear every little snuffle and whimper your sleep will be more disturbed than it need be.

● **with toddlers**
The important thing is to make going to bed a happy, relaxed time. Never force a child to bed as punishment — and then wonder why she resists going at sleeping time.

Sleep comes at different times

Boisterous romps just before bedtime don't exhaust a child; they're more likely to wind her up for more. End the day with a quiet story or nursery rhymes — good for both of you.

Time spent together before bed makes your child feel content and happy — and it saves time later. The toddler who feels cheated out of attention can make countless demands after lights out.

Try not to leave bedtime until you are both at the end of your tether. Give a warning that playing has to stop and begin the going-to-bed steps while you're still on top of things. (And if she's really tired and grizzley at the end of a day and her clothes are dry and not too grubby, why not let her flop in them? Pyjamas don't really matter!)

Routine, especially about going to bed, becomes really important to most toddlers. Kisses in a certain order, toys arranged a special way, a teddy or cuddly tucked in beside her . . . they're not just delaying tactics. This is the stage when change is upsetting and she likes everything to be in its place.

The "just one more" calls of a two-year-old can drive you mad after a tiring day. So, if you've been through the rituals and seen to reasonable requests, don't feel guilty when you firmly say "No more" and refuse to go back. You'll do more damage by letting yourself get too hassled and uptight.

Going to sleep?

If a child's not sleepy, leave her with books or toys on her bed. You can't force her to sleep. But you want her in bed for your sake — and there's no harm in that. A regular bedtime is a good thing.

Early waking is a real bugbear and there's no way you can stop it. All you can do is encourage the toddler to stay in her room. Toys and books and maybe some food (a banana, or crackers or an apple for toddlers used to them) at the end of the bed help delay the evil hour when the whole family is woken.

Even the best sleepers wake in the middle of the night at times. Teething is often blamed but no-one really knows why children do it. If you're lucky, your toddler will talk and play and sing

to herself for a while and then drop off again. Don't go in or do anything about it. It's a normal, common pattern.

Firm, no-nonsense handling

It's worse when she calls or cries out, or gets up and creeps into your bed. If you don't mind a small warm body in bed with you, let her stay. Or you may find it best to have a short snuggle and then firmly return the wanderer to her own bed. Sometimes a drink and being tucked up again will do the trick.

The main thing is not to be playful, or she'll want more. The middle of the night is a time for firm, no-nonsense handling. If you've checked and comforted the child there'll be times when you feel so desperate with tiredness it's better to go back to your bed, even if the toddler still cries. At least give her that chance to settle. And remember, no-one is expected to be smiling round the clock, so don't feel guilty.

If parents share tucking a child into bed, or the night checking, it prevents a toddler getting hooked on having the same person every time — much better for everyone's sake.

Broken nights don't last forever. In the tough months you may have to adjust your sleep, going to bed early or resting during the day whenever junior does (far better than doing housework). You can't expect a baby not to interfere with your lifestyle — and it's in the early months that parents are the ones who have to do the adjusting.

Marching orders

25

The great food fuss

There isn't a normal child around who would let himself starve. Yet fuss over food makes whole families miserable meal after meal.

Babies vary

From the start, babies vary in their needs and growth rates — from day to day, week to week. Some babies will drink and eat everything they're offered; others have firm likes and dislikes. Some like nothing but milk for six or nine months; others like solids after a drink from about four months. There is no one pattern.

The first year is the time of greatest growth. You grow more then than at any other time of your life. Appetites are usually good.

Toddlers need less to eat

When the growth rate slows, often around nine months, so does the need for food. A baby who has loved eating starts pushing food away. Even a toddler on the trot all day seems to need less food than he used to.

Hassles begin when a mother doesn't realise this and when her child stops eating she starts worrying. Then begins the wheedling and coaxing and begging and threatening and bribing and fooling and fuming and nagging and fussing . . .

The battle you can't win

But there are some battles you can never win. It's best to dodge them altogether. You cannot force food into an unwilling child. He can always spit or vomit it out. No amount of fussing or fuming will change that. And it will never help your child enjoy eating.

Food forcing is the commonest cause of feeding 'problems'.

Even the best of eaters in infancy become finnicky at times. A child who likes bananas one meal may send them flying the next. Or he may eat up well in the mornings but want nothing for dinner. It might drive you wild, but it's normal.

And the good news is: It won't last! Fads usually pass quite quickly, if you can just shrug them off. Only if you let yourself get frantic over food and start wheedling, then growling, then punishing, will the problems grow. And they can seem to last a lifetime!

Just think of the antics grown-ups go through to force a spoonful through unwilling lips: dancing jigs, being dive-bombers, neighing like horses, pleading "Just one more to please the puppy — or grandma, or Santa Claus, or for the refugees in Bangladesh." No wonder the little tyrant keeps it all going by refusing to surrender and eat.

No help wanted

The danger is that it won't foster a liking for food, but it will encourage junior to hold the fort to get lots of attention. While appetites are changing, remember that your baby is wanting to do things for himself. It's not only food, but help he is pushing away.

Think what fun it must be to squeeze spaghetti through your fingers or stretch it out before stuffing it down! The mess may be horrific, but the baby left to dig his fingers in his dinner as soon as he can sit up and hold things will be quicker at coping without spills in the long run.

And, more important, he'll learn to eat just what he needs and no more. Some toddlers have problems through eating too much, not too little. Fat babies sometimes make fat adults.

Stop fussing

One of the best things for third or fourth children is that Mum is far too busy to fuss over every mouthful. So think of that — and relax!

The real need is to stop yourself worrying, rather than trying to make your child eat. If he's full of bounce and growing, even slowly, you can be sure he's getting enough to suit him, if not to please you.

Doesn't she realize I'm not hungry

When the food fights are on

If you feel already caught up in fuss and games over food, there are some things you can do:

- Resolve not to talk about food. Avoid "Eat up, One more to please Daddy. One for the pussy. One for you."
- Keep helpings really small. Make little sandwiches, tiny cubes of cheese, short carrot sticks. And don't fuss over clean plates — that idea means nothing to a child. If you're bothered about waste, eat it yourself!
- Make meals look good. How would you like the same dreary-looking mush every day? Remember older babies and toddlers need to learn to chew (chop bones and corn-on-the-cob are good, but watch for choking).
- Let your youngster feed himself. Newspapers or plastic under the highchair help with the mess.
- Give meals you have not spent ages preparing. Tinned baby food is fine, or adapt things from the family pot. If you haven't spent precious energy and time, you are less likely to flare up if your little darling spits it out.

- If you can't resist coaxing (and of course it's hard not to) try a picture book or story at meal time. Not "If you eat up, I'll read", but to create a relaxed atmosphere and take *your* eyes and mind off measuring mouthfuls.
- Make no fuss if what's offered is not eaten. But don't feel you have to give something else five minutes later. Remember, your child won't let himself starve.
- Don't threaten or punish over food. If it's taken for granted that hungry children eat, there's nothing naughty about not wanting to at times. Don't turn eating into a duty or 'good' behaviour.
- If mess and manners bother you, don't have junior join you at the table until you can cope. Tensions there ruin meals for the whole family.
- Try to make meals a treat sometimes so eating is seen as a pleasure. Candles on the table make magic for toddlers — or at least mean a party. With a bit of luck, they may respond by eating up.
- Have picnic meals — outside in the summer, on a big rug or old tablecloth by the fire in winter. Saves lots of hassle and mess.
- Snacks are important for little bodies which aren't adjusted to three big meals a day. Give things that are good for children to eat — fruit or crackers and peanut butter — and lots of drink. How often do parents go with nothing between meals?
- Let junior 'help' in getting ready for dinner, putting things on the table, maybe stirring something in a bowl, finding salt or sauce.
- If things have got really bad, try putting a day's supply of snacks *(make sure they are not just sweet biscuits or lollies)* and drinks in a low cupboard, stick on a colourful picture and tell your child to help himself. Don't even look to check what's gone. He won't starve!

Keep helpings really small

Good things to eat

Your nurse or doctor will help you decide on baby's first solids. Once he
is eating different foods, these are things that are good for growing children
to eat:

· Meat, fish, chicken, eggs, cheese, milk.
· Fresh fruit, fresh vegetables. Tinned baby foods.
· Bread, rice, porridge.

Snacks for toddlers

Dates, apple pieces, carrot sticks, cheese, crackers or bread with meat extract
or peanut butter, bananas, oranges.

Things that are bad if that's all a child eats

Chips, lollies, sweet biscuits, chocolate, cordial and fizzy drinks, doughnuts
and cakes, greasy take-aways.
Peanuts are DANGEROUS. They can get stuck on the way down!

The great pot battle

There's a heap of rubbish talked about 'potty training'. Mostly it's 'parent-training' that needs to be done. A baby left alone will train herself.

Here's another area where battles begin and bad feelings grow, simply through not knowing how a child develops.

Babies have no control
First, the facts: It is physically impossible for a baby to control her bladder and bowels until the nerve pathways linking them to the brain develop. Often this doesn't happen until around the second birthday. Boys are usually later with this development than girls. And it has nothing to do with intelligence!

Don't expect too much too soon
Problems start when too much is expected too soon.

So what about the mother who smugly smiles and tells you she hasn't had a dirty nappy in weeks — and her baby hasn't had her first birthday yet?

It means the mother has trained herself. She's learnt when her baby fills her nappy — and holds her over the pot at the right moment.

The baby uses it. But not because she's 'trained'. There's still a lot of learning ahead before she can respond to her own signals.

'Trained' toddlers are still learning
Trouble is that any mother who has avoided dirty nappies because of lucky timing is likely to be upset when, as almost always happens, her toddler shows her will and goes through a stage of refusing to sit on the pot.

Naturally, it's hard not to let these feelings show. And that sets up difficulties.

Dodge the battle
The best way to dodge the battles is to wait until your child starts telling you when she's wet or dirtied her nappy. In the summer around the second birthday leave nappies off at the beach or in the garden so she can see and feel what happens.

At the same time show her a potty, let her sit on it, play with it (first thing most kids do is wear it for a hat!) — but never force her to stay on it.

Explain what it's for and when she wets, or tells you she has, suggest she tries the pot.

Praise for successes — ignore mistakes
Toddlers learn faster with praise than with nagging or smacks. So beam when the pot is used, make light of the mistakes.

All children learn by copying, so leave the bathroom door open and let her see the rest of the family. Older children can often be the best teachers — and let parents off lots of hassle.

Little boys, and little girls too, love to copy Dad so provide a stool for them to stand on. (But don't worry if your son wants to sit to wee — it won't last till school!)

When it comes to progressing off the pot (some never use one) remember that being perched up on the big seat can be quite frightening. Not only can you fall off it — you might get washed away! Little seats can be helpful, or a stool or box for feet to feel firm on.

"I want to be alone"

Even in the freest households, toddlers suddenly want privacy sometimes. So if she wants the door shut and insists on wiping her own bottom, don't interfere. It's better to have slightly-soiled pants to wash than to hang round months longer than necessary.

Make a game of "And now we wash our hands" right from the start and this will become routine even when she's on her own — that's what 'training' is all about.

Mothers who do nothing except leave clothes off and produce a pot are not lazy or 'dirty'. They're the ones who most often report that suddenly their child trained herself. Ignore advice on foolproof 'methods' and explain to grandparents who did things differently why you are waiting.

Remember, it's not a mark of 'good' mothering if your baby is pot trained early. Nor is your toddler 'bad' or 'dirty' if she is slower than most.

When a battle has begun

Sometimes, because of the fuss that's been made, a child feels that poohing is naughty and nasty. She doesn't know that it is going on the floor or in her pants that makes Mum mad and, hoping to please, will hold on till it's too late. Then there's another accident, more fuss, and things get worse.

Or the holding-on leads to constipation and the child doesn't go for days on end. This causes pain when she eventually does go and leads to more holding-in to avoid more pain. A baby tin of prunes might help. Or you might need to talk to your nurse or doctor to help break the vicious circle.

Stay relaxed

The main thing is to stay relaxed about the whole business. Certainly don't punish accidents with shrieks and smacks.

Of course you feel rotten if you find pooh smeared all over the cot or living room floor. But there's hardly a child alive who hasn't played in a dirty nappy — it's one of the joys of parenthood the TV ads don't show you!

You don't need to pretend you like it. But don't make the child feel she revolts you. If you feel really angry, try to keep the fuss aimed at the mess, not your child.

Dry nights come later

Children vary tremendously in staying dry all night and there's nothing much you can do to hasten the process. It has nothing to do with laziness or naughtiness. Don't expect dry nappies at night too soon — it often takes until well into the third year and boys take longer than girls.

You can make sure your child goes to the lavatory before bedtime. And if she still takes a bottle to bed, cut down the amount of fluid in it.

One in six children are still bed-wetting when they start school. So don't think you've got a 'problem' if your three-year-old still does it.

Discipline—what does it really mean?

Discipline needn't be such a bugbear if you think of it as helping a child to help herself . . . to help her learn to live and play happily with others, to explore safely, to cope with feelings, to know what she can do, to develop interests.

It's not simple. There is no magic 'right' way. The way you discipline or teach your child depends on all the special qualities that make your family different from any other.

Discipline is not forcing a child to do what you want — you can't force a child to be 'good'. Of course smacks and shouts will stop a toddler doing something you don't like, but they won't teach her to do things you do like.

Children are never so naughty as when parents are miserable or tense or going through a low. Look at yourself now and then: Is your toddler extra boisterous and cheeky today? Or have you lost your sense of humour? Did you belt her because she deliberately spilt paint — or because Dad was late home from work?

Most parents find third or fourth children need less 'disciplining', not that they are born better, but parents understand the early stages that don't last and can guide their toddlers through them. So, think of that — and relax!

Distractions can work wonders

These 'Do's' might help

- **Praise more than punish**
  Little ones like to please (most of the time). And they want to be noticed. If you reward behaviour you like, you'll get more of it to please you. A hug, a smile, showing interest in what they do — these are the best rewards. No need for lollies or new toys.

- **Be reasonable in what you expect**
  Lively toddlers simply don't understand ideas like 'tidy', 'hurry', 'quiet', 'wait', "Where are your manners?" Give them time and help to learn.

- **Keep "No" for when you really need it**
  Your child needs you to set limits. If 'anything goes' she'll be very confused and bewildered. But do decide what matters most. Your child will learn the rules quicker if there aren't too many of them. If you seem bogged down in endless nagging perhaps you are fussing over things that don't really matter.

- **Avoid battles you can't win**
  You can't force your child to eat and sleep and pooh exactly when and how you want her to. You don't gain anything in long-term discipline by creating battles of wills. Understanding how babies grow towards behaviour you like is not being weak.

- **Distract or try your own tricks whenever possible**
  It's usually easy to switch a little one's attention from something you don't like to a harmless thing to do. Distraction is not 'giving in' — it can work wonders. If she fiddles with the TV knobs, offer an old torch to play with. If she meddles with your makeup, give her bits and pieces in an old handbag.

- **Stick to your guns on what is important**
  Nagging and threats are hopeless. Toddlers quickly learn to ignore a constant stream of

"If you touch the TV I'll smack you" that never means a thing.

- **Try to be consistent**
  Of course this varies with your mood and patience. But don't hug your toddler for feeding the cat one day and shriek at her for spilling milk in the cat's saucer the next.
- **Think ahead to forestall trouble**
  It's far better to put precious pieces out of reach for a while than to nag about not touching them; better not to let balls in the living room than smack when something gets broken.
- **Relax about your 'mistakes'**
  Of course you'll wallop and yell when you didn't really need to. Don't fret over it. As long as the general atmosphere is happy and loving your child will catch the right feelings.
- **Give choices that suit you**
  Beware of saying "Do you want to go to bed now? Do you want to get your shoes on?" Far better to say "Do you want to put pyjamas on by the heater or your bed?" when you've decided it is bedtime.
- **Say you're sorry if you let fly for nothing**
  Don't be scared to tell your child if you feel tired or grumpy and have over-reacted. A hug or talk together soon gets over the rumpus — and it helps your child learn to say "sorry" one day.

- **Make punishment immediate**
  Never threaten to deal with something later, or keep punishment for the other parent. And remember if you smack a lot, you can only smack harder when things get worse. If you shout, you can only shout louder. Children react to different things — a stern face is enough punishment for some; isolation in an armchair or removing a toy works with others.

You can't force your baby to be good

Behaviour that bugs you

Tantrums

Temper tantrums are ghastly. But tantrums are normal. They are part of growing that all children go through.

Usually they happen between 18 months and three — when your child is trying himself out against you and the world, when he loves to say "no", when he's determined to do things his way.

First thing to know is: Tantrums don't last. The more you can ignore them, the sooner they'll stop.

The child who's always whizzing about, flat out not to miss anything, full of bounce and bravado, is the one likely to have most tantrums. Especially if his parents are strict or perfectionists, anxious about his every move, fearful of having a child who 'gets away with anything'.

The first full-scale tantrum can be quite frightening. Suddenly your little darling goes purple with rage, hurls the nearest thing to hand, stamps his feet, refuses to move or falls to the ground with fists flailing, all the time screaming loudly enough to alert the whole neighbourhood. If it happens in a supermarket or busy street you feel like walking away forever.

So what do you do?

As best as you can, ignore it. Don't scream back. Don't smack. Don't give in to the demand. Don't try to reason. Don't fuss.

If it's in public there's not much you can do but grin and bear it, try to distract junior and remove yourselves as fast as possible.

Don't feel you must be seen to be punishing the screamer. It won't help stop him. And anyone who's been through it will understand.

Obviously it's easier at home. Then you can just walk away. Or firmly pick the child up and put him in his room. "That noise hurts my ears," you might say, and walk away.

Without an audience the circus will flop. And don't talk about it later in front of the performer. If he finds himself the centre of attention everytime, he'll keep up the act.

The trouble with tantrums is they usually happen when you're both at the

end of your tether — after a hot trip to town; tiring for you, boring for your toddler. Or when you've spent all day mopping up messes, tripping over toys, cheerfully coping until all your patience has gone just when you need it most to get junior into bed.

But try to keep cool. It's really worth it.

Distraction is the best tactic, if you can think of something to switch his attention before the full force of the tantrum builds up.

Dance a jig (not so good in the supermarket!), swoop down to pick something up and pretend to hide it, rush and look out the window — anything to stop junior in full cry.

It's not a matter of 'giving in'. You can't force a child out of a tantrum. They are a phase that won't last. You won't be starting bad habits if you gently guide him through.

Best of all, think ahead. If you have a long shopping trip ahead take a paper bag with a drink or snack or favourite toy. If you know he likes to dress himself or clamber into the car unaided, don't bundle him along. Try to leave that extra time for his slower ways.

And when the storm of a tantrum is over, reassure with a cuddle or quiet time together — he may have been scared by the force of his own fury. Don't give any lollies or whatever he was shrieking for — just a little of yourself.

Then think about what caused it all. Was it really necessary to stop him — or were you in a hurry? Was he really doing damage — or couldn't you bear the sight of another mess?

Hitting, biting, scratching

It's awful for everyone when children are constantly bickering. But while they're learning to play together you have to expect some fights. All toddlers hit and scratch and maybe bite at times. They don't have a lot of other ways to quarrel.

Remember, your toddler needs you to set limits. Of course you won't want to ignore it if your child is beating up another — or being beaten up.

Judging when to step in to sort out the scraps can be tricky. There's no need to interfere with every little spat; the children learn to sort a lot out themselves.

But when you do intervene, try not to over-react — a big fuss from a grown-up often leads to more hitting, not less. Realise that what looks terrible to adult eyes doesn't mean the same to a two-year-old.

If you do catch a child about to hit, quietly stop him. Holding his arm firmly while you say, "No, you mustn't do that, it hurts," should work. Or if he's worked up to a rage, remove him from playing for a short while.

Step in and divert wherever possible. This is always better than entering a battle of wills. It's not a matter of being soft; at this stage toddlers can easily be sidetracked into a new game and given time for tempers to cool.

You can never be sure who started a fight so don't try to sort it all out. And don't be harder on your own child than on the visitor, or on the oldest all the time. Often mothers, anxious that their child should be 'nice' and have friends, come down heavily every time their own toddler makes a move. It isn't always your child's fault when a visiting little one cries!

Toddlers learn by copying. If shouts and slaps are used at home to settle arguments, that's what will be used with play mates.

And often, if you've just scolded or smacked, your toddler will turn round and take it out on someone smaller. Bad feelings can run right through a family or play group.

Biting is really upsetting — a little ring of red tooth marks in a small arm is a horrid sight. Lots of people think it's a good idea to bite back, to show the biter how it feels. But that really just shows that big people can do things children are not allowed to do. Or, if mum and dad can bite, won't he think it's okay for him too?

Better to remove the biter from playing for a while. Try to tell him, he's okay, but biting isn't. Never ever! Don't be too harsh, even if you're horrified.

Breaking, smashing, wall scribbling

All little children break things and make messes.

Often natural energy and curiosity get a child into far more trouble than he can understand.

A toddler who reaches up to feel something on a table, pulls a cloth and brings dishes crashing down, is not being 'naughty'. There's no way he could know what would happen. (A defiant yank when he's older is a different matter.)

Crawling babies don't start by being deliberately destructive. They just want to explore everything.

The best way to cut down accidents and wilful wrecking is to accept the fact you have a wham-banging, mess-making creature on your hands for a while and gear your house accordingly. It's only for a short time really.

See there are spaces for play. A child who's always hearing, "No, no, you mustn't touch. You can't do that here", will break out more than the one given space to move, make messes and let off steam. Or she may just seem more destructive because there's so much around to hurt.

Naturally, you don't want mud pies on your carpet or balls thrown at your china — but is there anywhere to do these things?

If there's space to set up toys, children learn that you too have spaces you want for yourselves.

If there's a garden to run and jump in, there's no need to do it on the bed. If you live in a tiny flat it's hard. Then you have to make more effort to find space — in a park, at a play centre, walking together on a footpath.

If there's a blackboard or newsprint tacked up to draw on then other walls can be out-of-bounds.

If there are newspapers or old magazines to crumple and rip into, the ones you still want can be kept intact.

If there are strong toys to bang, then the furniture needn't take a pounding.

A certain amount of aggression is not only normal — your child needs it to survive.

But if your toddler seems on the rampage with extra force and fierceness, maybe he's going through a stage of jealousy (is there a new baby in the house?), frustration because he can't do things (are there some skills he can handle?), or needs some extra attention (do you notice him only when he smashes something?).

Sex play

Children learn about sex from their parents, even if they are never talked to about it. The way you treat each other, the way you treat their bodies, the way you react when they play with themselves — it all affects their attitude to sex.

It's normal and natural for babies to be curious about their bodies, and those of all around them — brother, sister, friend, mum, dad. Why shouldn't they be?

As they explore with their fingers they find they get nice feelings from touching themselves. Baby boys often have erections when their nappies are off — it doesn't mean much and it's certainly nothing to worry about.

Masturbation has been a dirty word for so long, there are still lots of fears and false ideas about it. It is not harmful, it does not make people strange, it is not something perverted or shocking.

In fact, it is only if parents' reactions turn it into something a child feels tense and scared and guilty about that any harm can come of it.

If it upsets you to see toddlers touching or stroking or playing with themselves, or each other, realise it is your problem, not theirs. Don't turn it into something nasty for them by being heavy.

Treat sex play as you would if they were pointing or poking each other's ears, or eyes, tummies or toes. If they might hurt themselves, you'd stop them and gently explain that ears are precious and nothing must be poked into them.

Or if you feel uneasy because it's going on too long, switch the game with "And now let's see if it's stopped raining . . . let's look for letters . . . sing a song . . ."

A smack or growling or threats: "It'll drop off." "That's filthy, no-one will play with you." "Nice girls don't do that . . . " will only make the child fearful and ashamed.

And these tense feelings may lead to the opposite of what you want — more masturbation, not less. They may also be the start of lots of unhappiness in teenage and adult life.

If your child seems interested in nothing much else but his own body, that's a signal he's not getting enough warmth and affection from people, or other good things to do.

Do you have time to be with him? Does he have friends his own age to play with? Do you have cuddles, or read books or play ball together? Is he having fun with sand and mud and paint and dough? If you're worried, talk about it to your nurse, or your doctor, or a friend who seems relaxed and happy with her children.

Dirty ditties

Children love words. And even the sweetest little angels come up with some shockers.

At any time your toddler is likely to go through a "poohs and bums and wees" stage, squealing with delight at the actions or the words — especially if there are older brothers or sisters to egg him on.

If you react furiously, or too shocked, or laugh and tell all your friends, your child will find he has a brand new way of getting attention — and keep on and on and on.

So what do you do? *Relax*. The words hurt you more than the child. He won't use them for ever.

If some words really get at you try turning them into a rhyming game: "Dirty pig, curly wig, mighty big . . ." "Poohey bum, shiny drum, rolly tum . . ." Takes the sting out of it all, and helps children enjoy words.

Won't share

Most parents hate the idea of selfish children, so from the earliest chance they urge them to share, often expecting far too much too soon.

Before a child can share she has to learn what 'mine' means. The discovery of the magic word 'mine' is a big step in finding out about the world. It means there are some things she can move and control and keep. No wonder she wants to enjoy that stage a while.

Then a toddler learns some things are 'not mine', and this is often hard to accept for a while.

Learning about time is involved too. For a start everything is 'now' or 'not now'. Then she begins to understand 'soon', 'just for a minute', 'next'.

When the little ones start playing together they learn about the possibility of 'turns'. They learn that something that is 'mine' can go out of their hands, *and come back*.

Only when a toddler has been through these steps can she learn to share happily; she need no longer fear a toy will be taken away and disappear forever.

It doesn't take long, with lots of relaxed and gentle help. But if forced to share, a toddler is likely to panic and hold on even tighter to her things.

Don't expect too much of your 18-month-old. If she loves her teddy, why should she share it? Do you share your favourite vase?

Let your child own some things that are precious to her and let her decide if she'll share them.

Jealousy

In the rough and tumble of family life jealousy is often hard to handle.

The time most parents worry about is when a new baby is thrust upon the toddler used to having mum and dad and home and toys to herself.

You can't prevent all jealousy. But you can try to understand and avoid things that make it worse.

It's not naughtiness. It's another of those stages or feelings which are perfectly natural and, calmly coped with, won't last.

Children are taught about eyes, ears, nose and toes right from the start. But mostly we let the inside things, feelings, go unmentioned.

If your toddler is obviously jealous, this is a good chance to talk about feelings, to help her accept that good and bad feelings exist. "Yes, you're cross because Mummy spends so much time with the baby." "Yes, it's tough to wait." "Yes, it feels awful to be angry, doesn't it?" "You know Mummy and Daddy loved you first and still love you just as much . . . ."

He may be trying to be nice

38

DO

Talk to your toddler (even if she can't talk to you yet) about the new baby and what will happen — how busy you'll be and how she can help.

Make plans well in advance and if Dad and grandparents can't mind the firstborn, do try to let her get to know her minder.

Arrange for her to visit the hospital, or keep in touch by telephone. Have the baby 'give' a present to big brother or sister. Or perhaps arrange a swap.

Make special times or have a treat alone with the elder child to have some fun together, explaining that baby is still too young.

Include her when visitors fuss over the baby. It's easy to switch attention to the toddler — far better than waiting till outrageous antics force you to notice her.

Understand if your pot-trained toddler starts wetting or dirtying her pants again, sucks her thumb more, throws more tantrums, stops dressing herself, wants a bottle or breast again, hits other playmates.

Reassure with cuddles and extra attention. Ignore the baby behaviour and relax — it won't last.

DON'T

Don't be surprised if your toddler shows no interest or some nasty feelings to the baby. Remember, it takes time for her to love the new baby.

Don't make big changes just as the baby is born. Moves to a new bed, new room, new nursery or kindergarten should be made well before — or much later.

Don't feel the older child has to have a present every time baby gets one. With the right atmosphere she'll soon learn to cope.

Don't turn 'helping' into something she has to do.

Don't stop the toddler from holding the baby. It's amazing what the newborn can take!

Don't be too severe if she pokes or pinches the baby — she'll only sneak back for a harder go when you're not looking.

Don't compare behaviour. "Baby eats all her dinner . . . baby is a good girl." That only makes the first resentful.

Don't over-react if the toddler dumps a tip-truck of sand in baby's cot — she may be trying to be nice — or if she pushes the baby away from her toys harder than necessary. She may hurt baby without meaning to.

Involving Dad

We've written this book to try to help Mums and Dads understand and enjoy their baby more. Ideally, we wouldn't have to have a separate word about Dads, but we all know that mostly, in our society, Mum is the one at home, alone, with the baby.

Sadly, a lot of fathers have very little to do with their offspring, especially in the early years. Sometimes a father thinks he'll get to know his child when she's grown up a bit — only to find he's left it too late.

Sometimes a Dad shuts himself off from his baby — "That's women's work, I'm too much a man to be caught doing that" — and it's hard to change such a man's view.

Sometimes he feels left out, unable to break through the circle of females fussing round his baby — Mum, Grandma, nurses, neighbours.

Maybe he thinks it's better for him to work overtime to provide more for the baby — often things a baby doesn't really need.

Or perhaps he doesn't get a chance to do things his way so he can feel confident handling the baby. Lots of mothers turn off a willing Dad by always stepping in, coming between Dad and his baby, taking over when he's trying to pin on a nappy or help with a feed.

There may be lots of reasons why a new mother excludes Dad from being really close to his baby. Perhaps it was the baby, more than anything else, she wanted from the relationship. Perhaps she sees her 'job' as having to do everything for the baby; she feels guilty about stepping back to let others take a turn — even Dad.

But, commonly, it is just thoughtlessness that leads mothers into the trap of never giving Dad a chance to be really involved.

Right from the start, while everything is strange to both of you, it's good if you can learn together — share the stumbling, share the fun. If Mum keeps doing everything, Dad's not likely to insist he plays a part.

One of the best ways for a Dad to enjoy and help with the baby is for him to have time alone with her. Then there's no chance of him being told his way is no good. Even if it's only taking the baby for a walk in a pram or slung on his back, or, later, the bath-and-story-and-bedtime routine — wise mothers will stay well clear so there's no way they can interfere.

It's ridiculous for mothers to feel 'grateful' to a Dad who pitches in — whose baby is it, anyway?

Danger signals for babies

Although this book is mostly about feelings, there are some signs of sickness in babies that are so important we've listed them below. Of course with a new baby it is sometimes hard to know when to worry and when to relax — perhaps you could talk to your nurse or doctor about this list before baby shows any unusual reactions. It's often little things that worry new mothers the most, things they feel are too silly to ask anyone else. Remember, nothing is too trivial to ask about — anything that makes you anxious is important to you and your baby.

If you see any of these signs get help quickly:
* Raspy coughs, wheezes, or if baby finds it hard to breathe.
* Extra quick or grunting breathing — this needs urgent help.
* Baby refuses two normal feeds.
* Vomits or is sick more than once.
* Baby has several runny, extra-smelly poohs: Vomiting and diarrhoea together are serious. Babies lose water very quickly and it is *urgent to get medical help.* Sunken eyes and dry nappies show his water loss.
* Baby has an unusual, different-sounding cry for a long time — an hour or more.
* Baby is hard to wake up.
* Baby has a convulsion or 'fit'.
* Baby has a runny discharge coming from an ear, or pulls and rubs his ear a lot, maybe grizzling at the same time.
* Baby is unusually floppy, or extra hot, or extra cold, even without other signs of sickness.

If baby is not getting better 24 hours after a doctor has seen him, ask the doctor about him again. This is important.

If you are new to your area, discuss how to contact a doctor with your nurse, maybe try to see one, or ring and check with the doctor's nurse that you could go to the doctor, before you need to. Make sure you know what to do for

medical help in weekends too. Hopefully, you'll never need it!

Immunisation
Some of the worst diseases of childhood can now be avoided by having your baby protected against them with immunisation: whooping cough, diphtheria, poliomyelitis, measles and tetanus. Babies die, or can be severely damaged if they get these diseases. Be sure to protect your baby against them.

Polio vaccine is given by mouth, the others by injection. Your baby should go to the doctor at 3 months, 5 months, 12 months, 18 months and just before he starts school for these vaccinations.

Accidents
Far more babies are injured and die from accidents than from illness — keep your child safe from cars, fire, water, poisons. It's often a matter of life or death.

Danger signals for mums and dads

If your bad feelings outweigh the good, and seem to last longer and longer and get stronger . . .
If you can't face getting out of bed in the mornings. Not the normal drag of tiredness after broken nights, but real dread of coping with a new day . . .
If your baby seems to go on and on crying, night and day . . .
If you cry a lot, often for no reason . . .
If you have ghastly feelings of panic or despair when the baby cries; if you fear you might lose control and hit her, or try to smother the cries with a pillow . . .
If you can't think of any fun things to do with your child, can't get your mind off your miseries, your tiredness, your resentments . . .
If you feel utterly trapped, alone, can't talk to anyone because no-one else would understand . . .
If you feel a 'failure', think you must be a 'bad', unnatural person to feel this way as a parent . . .
If you think your baby would be better off without you . . .
If you find no pleasure in sex . . .

Especially dads
If you feel left out, just a useless spare part . . .
If you feel you're only a money machine that must grind on . . .
If you'd rather go to the pub every night than face home and kids . . .

Then you may need help. All these feelings are normal — in small doses! But if they seem to overwhelm you, to shut out everything else in your life, then you should try to talk about them. Depression, especially in the first few weeks for new mothers, is very common and your doctor may be able to help you. It won't do you — or your baby — any good to let bad feelings go on building up.

This is the time to help each other by accepting that these feelings are part of your new deal — but they won't last forever.

Maybe you are expecting too much, trying to be a perfect new parent, trying to please everybody — your baby, your partner, your self, the grandparents. It's too much.

When everything gets on top of you the effort of trying to break out of the mess may seem beyond you. But it's really worth it.

Don't think you must care for your baby 24 hours a day, seven days a week, single-handed. Everyone needs a break from routine, from a job that is very demanding — and there's nothing more demanding than a new baby.

Dad may be working overtime thinking he's doing his best to buy things that are vital — but are they really urgent needs? Better to sit on boxes a bit longer if he could come home earlier and take the baby for a walk or share the end-of-the-day routine.

Think about what you really enjoy that you haven't done since the baby was born. Is it going to the movies? Meeting friends for a drink? Walking along a beach? A hobby or job the baby has squeezed out of your life?

Arrange a baby sitter and get away from it all, ideally to have some fun with each other, or maybe to have time on your own. If there are willing grandparents around you'll be doing them — and your baby — a good turn by letting them be alone together. If you can find friends to swap baby-sitting with you'll be starting something good for the years ahead. And if you have to pay, go without something else — new things can wait but you and your baby need the break now.

If the danger signals are really worrying you, tell your nurse. There are people in every community who understand, who may be able to help.

It may not be easy to find just the right person but no-one can guess how rotten you feel if you keep trying to hide it. The first step may be the hardest of all — to say, "I can't bear it all. Yes, I want some help." There's no reason to be ashamed. Becoming a parent is a big shock to the system and it isn't all lovely by any means. Probably you never dreamed you'd be feeling like this. Don't judge yourself a 'failure'. Don't look at others who seem capable — they may be hiding their feelings too.

Go through the list of addresses at the back of this book. There'll be someone to turn to.

Time off—time apart

Your baby may be the most important thing in your life but don't let her become the only important thing.

Babies grow up and leave you behind; you have them for only a small part of your life. Babies will take all the time and energy and attention and loving you can give — but they don't need you to give up everything else for them.

You matter, your feelings count; your relationships and interests are as important as being a parent.

If all your life revolves around your children, all your hopes and plans are pinned on them, you're bound to be disappointed. It's far too big a load for them to carry.

And children have to learn that the world doesn't spin round them; they're part of a family where everyone's feelings count.

For many years you are their window on the world; they see it all through your eyes. Your activities and interests outside home broaden their horizons.

Trouble is that when your baby needs you most — in the first three years — that's the time when you most need a break now and then.

Nobody can be a 'good' parent 24 hours a day, smiling, gentle and caring from dawn to dark and often all through the night as well. There are lots of times when it's better for you and your baby to have a break apart.

If you feel driven mad with being shut up alone to cope with children day in, day out, or feel very resentful or bored, you won't be doing anyone much good.

Play groups
One of the best ways to get time off for yourself — and do something really good for your child — is to get a little play group going in your own neighbourhood.

So you're a stranger? So are lots of other new mothers probably. Try talking to someone with a baby the same size as yours in your street, or ask the nurse if she knows anyone.

You may feel too shy at first but see the organisations listed at the back of this book and check if any are in your district, they could help you.

Once you get to know each other — and it doesn't take long with little ones — you can take it in turns to have two or three or four children to play while the other mums have a break. Or have two mums 'on duty', two off.

Great for you, great for the children.

To work, or not to work?
All mothers work a lot. Some have jobs outside the home as well — because they have to; because they want to. Some mothers keep on breast-feeding while back at work, some wean to go back to work, others put off taking a job until all their children are at school. There is no one way . . .

The big question is: What is best for your child when you are apart? This may be one area where advice from all around really confuses you.

Because all babies are different, each one is ready to do different things at different times. Some are happy to be left long before others; some are up and off over the garden fence while others still sit in the backyard.

You have to decide what's best for yourself and your baby. Modern mothers can feel guilty whatever they choose to do but try not to feel guilty about your decision. Ignore others' remarks. If you feel too anxious, your child will pick it up and think something *is* wrong.

Day care
If you plan to have someone else mind your

How would you like to meet strangers every day?

child, try to let them get to know each other gradually before you leave.

If you're lucky, perhaps you can find someone to come to your house — maybe another mother who will bring her baby or toddler with her. Or try to find a neighbour or mother at home with her own children who is happy to have one more to earn some extra money. Your health nurse may know of someone suitable.

Good day care is having someone who cares, someone who does more than just feed and change and watch your child.

If your child is going to a nursery or day care centre, it's best if there aren't too many children for each person to look after. And aim for the fewest changes in staff. How would you like to meet a stranger every day?

The first step in search of good day care may be a bit scary for you, as well as your child, especially if you have to work and feel you have few choices.

Do talk to the nursery supervisor. It's important for you to get to know each other so you can share understanding of your child.

Can you talk to her easily? Does she, and her staff, say "hullo" and take a real interest in the children there? Is there space for play? Space for quiet, or a sleep? Do the children seem relaxed and happy, buzzing into fun activities?

These are just a few of the questions that might help you choose. If the nursery is excessively quiet and tidy or excessively boisterous and chaotic, and if you feel awkward or see that no-one really listens and talks to the children, try to find somewhere else.

Good day care can help you both in many ways. It's worth trying to find the best available.

Housework

Are you a career house-cleaner? Do you dust and tidy and polish and sweep because you need to — for your house's sake, or for your sake? Do you do more than you have to because there's nothing else for you to do? Because you think the neighbours expect it?

The best way to get time off is to cut down on housework. Stick to the essentials, try to do them early in the day before you're tired, and leave the rest.

Sit on the couch, and play with your baby, instead of vacuuming under it. Take her for a walk in the pram when you're on edge about the work — lovely for you both and out of sight of the work that worries you!

Don't clean the floor if you know there'll be toddlers in and out from a sandpit. Remember, there's nothing dirty about toys — they don't need to be cleaned away all the time.

A quick whisk around at the end of the day, biffing toys into boxes, can have the same effect as hours of work.

And if friends call at night and you're bothered by the dust or debris, light some candles and turn the lights off. Saves energy — yours and the country's! Looks fun. Hides the mess!

When you hit too hard

Lots of new and strange feelings come with a baby; while you're learning about the baby you find out a lot about yourself too.

It's like the old nursery rhyme: *When it's good, it's very very good, but when it's bad, it's horrid.*

One of the most horrid and frightening things to discover is how angry and upset your baby can make you feel — how you even hate her at times. That's a feeling not many people admit to, so it can come as a real shock.

The popular myth is that all mums and dads love their children all the time — anyone who doesn't must be some kind of monster!

When you feel resentful and angry about your baby, more bad feelings pile on top — shame and guilt that you feel that way. ''What kind of a person am I? I must be rotten to hate my own kid. . . .''

Maybe you feel quite pannicky at the thought, or try to pretend it never existed. Shut it out, bottle it away. .

Everyone has bad feelings, bad days with children. It's sad, but nothing can be so infuriating as your own child. It doesn't mean you don't love her; strong feelings — good and bad — show you really do care.

Life can be tough enough without a grizzley, demanding two-year-old constantly at your side. If you're worrying about money, and a leaking roof, and a neighbour has complained about the noise, and you had a row at breakfast, and a friend's forgotten your birthday, and you break a full bottle of milk at the gate . . . your toddler's crayoning on the walls can be the last straw.

Wham! You bash her far harder than you meant to. And then feel like hell.

Baby bashing upsets everyone. Some say they find it impossible to imagine how it could happen. But most parents, if they're honest, know there are moments they'd like to forget, times when they felt out of control, when they flung a

Words hurt too

child away too hard, or hit out with far more force than they meant.

Extra hard wallops can be damaging. But children get emotionally battered by a constant hammering of growls and threats, shouts and scorn — by being told they're no good, just a damn nuisance. Those unseen scars are even harder to heal than bruises or broken arms.

Perhaps you're scared of how desperate you feel sometimes. But what can you do
- if you have more bad and unhappy feelings about your baby than good ones . . .
- if you know you're smacking or hitting your child too hard and too often . . .
- if you feel you can't stop growling and picking on your toddler . . .
Then, you need help.

Of course it won't be easy. Especially if you already feel very alone. Perhaps you're a solo parent, or don't know the neighbours or have any friends. Perhaps you don't like your health nurse or feel you can't talk to her or your doctor.

But there are more and more people around who do understand these problems. There is help available, though it may take a lot of guts before you admit you need it.

That's the first step: Admitting you need help.

No-one can guess you're desperate if you refuse to let on. Don't let shame stop you. It's silly to think that "Everyone else seems to cope, so why shouldn't I?" Remember, there's no such creature as a perfect parent who never has ugly thoughts.

Try talking to your nurse if you feel okay with her. She may be able to help, or know someone else who can — perhaps a minister, or a counsellor or social worker from your local hospital, Family Planning or Citizens Advice Bureau; maybe an understanding mother.

Look at the addresses at the back — you might find help is not as far away as you feared.

Even talking about it to a friend might take some of the pressure off. And let someone mind your baby to give you a break.

Parents who batter their babies are not always the ones who couldn't care less or who neglect their kids. Often it's because they so desperately longed to have a baby to love them that they can't bear it when the baby cries and cries, or the toddler has tantrums and refuses to eat. They hoped for too much too soon — and broken hopes lead to frantic feelings.

Whatever the reasons behind the violent feelings, the worst thing is to pretend they don't exist. Or let them build up until they burst out.

When sex turns you off

Making love while the baby is growing inside you is fine, unless your doctor has told you not to for some specific reason.

Some women enjoy sex more than ever when they're pregnant; others not so much. Some men are turned on by the bulge; others switch off.

Whatever your feelings, it's important to talk about them, even if your sex life is not great in these months.

Warmth and affection mean a lot when a woman is going through the big changes before and after birth. A cuddle and hug may mean more than making love for a while. Don't feel bad about letting your man know this; he too may be a bit unsure in his new role. It's sad if you miss out on the affection because you're afraid it will lead to sex.

After birth, many new mothers find sex leaves them cold — maybe just for a few weeks, sometimes longer. Fathers too sometimes feel diffident about sex while they get used to their lover having become a mother.

For lots of couples, a baby arrives before they've had a chance to sort themselves out sexually. It can take years to have a really good and exciting sex life — that's something movies and magazines don't talk about.

If you're having a bad time in bed don't think you're on your own. It's a very common scene but it's not part of life and loving that many people are prepared for.

Disappointment can quickly lead to frustrations and resentment and feelings of 'failure' and despair that make couples react against each other. So the difficulties get worse.

The main thing is to try to keep in touch with each other's feelings. Talk and be patient. Like broken nights, this stage shouldn't last!

It may help to talk about some of the reasons why sex turns you off for a while:

Pain
It may be painful if you try to make love too soon after birth, especially if stitches were necessary.

And fear of pain leads to anxiety the next time and so tensions start a vicious circle. How soon is too soon? Before a woman feels relaxed and ready — it may be a week, it may be a month after birth.

Exhaustion
You're never so busy as in the first few months with a new baby. It's all so strange and a little scary and after the excitement of bringing home the baby life seems one long round of one more job that has to be done. On top of it all you never get a decent night's sleep because the little darling keeps calling for more. It's exhausting. It's hard enough to be a good mother round the clock — but sexy too? It just doesn't seem possible.

Hormones
Hormones are the chemical messengers that affect all the body's responses. They are active in all the changes of birth and breast feeding and often take a while to settle down. Once periods start again regularly the hormone balance should be returned to normal. But until then, the effect of the turmoil may be to turn a woman off sex.

Some breast-feeding mothers enjoy sex immensely, others don't enjoy it at all. There's no knowing how your body will respond. The milk that leaks upsets some couples, though it is a turn-on for others. There's no reason to be embarrassed — it's normal and natural. Trouble is, we hardly ever think of breasts for their feeding function.

New responsibilities
After being free and spontaneous as lovers, suddenly you both have a changed scene: someone else to think of, who never goes away and who's ill-timed demands must be met. If you're aware of the baby's every snuffle beside you, or always listening for a cry, sexy feelings hardly get a chance.

Put the baby in another room and try to forget him for a while

Fear of becoming pregnant

No matter how delighted you both are with the baby, the thought of another one right away probably fills you with horror. Breast feeding is *not* absolutely sure to prevent you becoming pregnant again. Contraception is best discussed with your doctor or at a family planning clinic (see end page) because there may be some problems with using the pill, or injection, or IUD or diaphragm straight after birth. A condom and jelly may be best for a few weeks.

New role resentments

If you have been used to working with other people and being respected for the job you do, or if you and your man have shared earning and home responsibilities, you might find it hard being home alone with the baby, especially if you're suddenly expected to take over all the jobs you used to share. If your man takes no special notice of you till you flop exhausted into bed, resentments are bound to grow.

Fathers often feel pushed aside when a new baby comes home to rule the roost (as they inevitably do for the first few weeks). Instead of feeling he's gained a child, many a man feels he's lost a lover.

Talk about how you feel before resentments build up.

Fear of failure

Once you get anxious about love-making it's impossible to relax and enjoy it. If every touch makes you rigid with wondering, "Why don't I turn on?" "When will the juices flow?" "How will I ever come?" things will only get worse.

Try to enjoy each touch or moment of closeness as it happens, not worrying about what it may lead to. Above all, try to talk to each other.

It's not a matter of one mate's 'failure' — just a difficult time that you have to work through together.

HELP!
how to get it

Health Visitor

Your Area Health Authority Visitor normally visits new babies about the tenth day after delivery. If you have been discharged from hospital after forty-eight hours, the midwife will visit you daily up to the tenth day.

You do not have to contact the Health Visitor: the Area Health Authority arranges that she should call. You may have met her before at your ante-natal clinic, or she may have come to visit you at home before the birth. In some cases the Health Visitor is the midwife who delivered the baby.

Your Health Visitor can be contacted through your local child health clinic or your doctor's surgery and your district nursing officer.

Child Health Clinic

Your Health Visitor can advise on all matters of child health and will put you in touch with your local Child Health Clinic. These in fact go under a number of names, such as well-baby, child welfare, or family health clinics. Some local authorities provide Day Nurseries for under-fives and most take a limited number of young babies.

Hospital — Ambulance

In an emergency — if your baby is burned or swallows pills or poisons or has a bad fall — go to the casualty department of your nearest hospital. Call an ambulance — dial 999 — if you have no car and the accident is serious. Try to remember to take the container or sample of poisonous substance your child has swallowed.

While your child is in hospital, try to stay with him or her as much as possible, even overnight.

Family Planning

The Family Planning Association has a network of clinics which provide a free contraceptive service. In addition they will help with advice about fertility problems, vasectomy and psychosexual counselling.
Headquarters: 27-35 Mortimer St, London, W 1. 01 636 7866

National Childbirth Trust

As part of its work of education for parenthood, the Trust runs a Breastfeeding Promotion Group who help women breastfeed successfully, with local supporters for each area where possible.
Headquarters: 9 Queensborough Terrace, Bayswater, London W 2. 01 229 9319

Citizens' Advice Bureaux

Look in your phone book for your local C.A.B. It can direct you to all helping agencies, tell you what benefits or help may be available through government departments, advise on legal or money problems, direct you to child care centres, play centres, kindergartens, or counselling or guidance services.

Kith and Kids

Self-help group of parents with handicapped children.
Headquarters: Bedford House, 35 Emerald St, London W C 1. 01 504 3001

Samaritans

Offer a telephone help service to those who are in distress and may be feeling desperate. See local telephone book for number.